DESIGNS-

and HOW TO USE THEM

745

By JOAN B. PRIOLO

STERLING PUBLISHING CO., Inc.
New York

In the British Empire:
W. H. ALLEN, London

DEDICATED TO

Tony, Carl and Chris, who have suffered long and patiently
through the preparation of this book.

Photographs by Joseph De Caro

Second Printing, January 1958

Library of Congress Catalog Card No.: 56-7696

© Copyright, 1956
by Sterling Publishing Company, Inc.
The Sterling Building, New York 10, N. Y.

TABLE OF CONTENTS

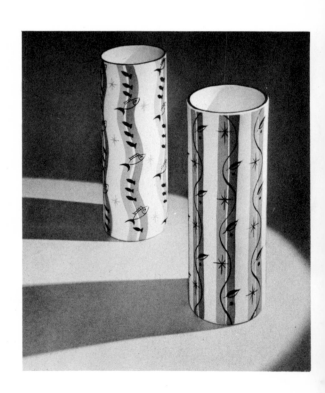

HOW TO USE THIS BOOK

In our highly mechanized society today, more and more people are turning to arts, crafts, and hobbies in their desire for personal expression.

Because the trend to creative expression is of the greatest benefit to both the individual and society, we have tried to encourage it as much as possible with the designs, color techniques, and suggestions in this book. Hobbyists, craftsmen, artists and students can express themselves more satisfactorily in their craft by the use of interesting techniques and good designs.

We start you off with a Glossary of methods and descriptions of the techniques of decorating in all the various craft fields. In the rest of the book, the particular techniques are not repeated, but are designated by **bold face type** so that you may refer back to the Glossary (on Pages 6 to 11) for a complete description until you become familiar with the technical details. The methods offered are simple in procedure, but unique and professional in effect!

Next you are shown in text and picture which methods are most suitable for your particular field, hobby or project. This section continues with suggestions as to the most suitable paints, materials and backgrounds, as well as the types of designs most appropriate to each method of decorating.

The remainder of the pages are filled with designs of every type and size. At the bottom of each design page is a simple color key, complete with background suggestion, to help you further in your decorating. This key is intended only as a guide, so don't be afraid to exercise your own ideas of color and methods.

Because simplicity in design and color is the basis of effective decorating, the designs are neither elaborate nor intricate. They do not require any knowledge of complicated painting techniques. Consequently, you can easily adapt them to any craft.

All the items shown in the photographs were done entirely with the designs and methods presented in this book, thus illustrating in color and in black-and-white the finished results of applying these ideas and designs to your decorating.

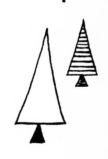

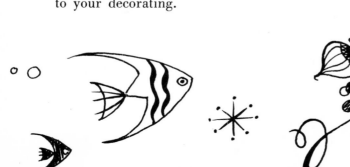

GLOSSARY
of Techniques

COLLAGE—As referred to in this book, collage consists of photos or clippings pasted on an original line drawing to produce an incongruous effect.

ENLARGE—To enlarge a drawing, first rule the original drawing into squares. Decide how large a design you want. Then, on another sheet of paper, lay out the larger area and rule in the same number of squares. Then copy the lines in each square as ruled in the original drawing.

NEWSPAPER MASKS — This simple procedure is effective on paper, wood, ceramics, and metal. Transfer the main outline of your design to newspaper and cut it out. This is your mask. Using glycerine (available at any drug store), "paste" the mask on the surface to be decorated. Glycerin is just tacky enough to keep the mask in place, but is not a paste and is easy to remove.

Spatter, spray or sponge your paint (or other medium) around the mask, going well over the edges of the mask to make certain of a sharp outline. When the paint is *thoroughly* dry (in the case of lacquer or ceramic paint this will be only a minute or two) remove the paper mask. You can use any sharp tool to pry up the edges of the newspaper. If there is still some wet glycerin remaining, wipe it off with a cloth before decorating

Spatter around and over the newspaper mask. Then remove the mask.

Hand strokes complete the design.

further. Then you are ready for your detail work.

This technique is professional and simple. If you are using a design as a repeat or double, cut more than one paper mask at a time.

PUMICE POWDER—For an extra fine finish on wood or metal (which has been previously varnished) soak a rag with crude oil and sprinkle it with pumice powder. Rub the varnished surface gently with the rag until it starts to feel smooth. Then wipe off all excess powder with turpentine. When the surface is completely free of grit, varnish again and repeat the rubbing process.

SCRATCHBOARD — This technique is used mainly for reproduction purposes. Scratchboard is a heavy paper with a white clay coating.

You ink the scratchboard with black india ink and scratch out your design with a sharp tool. The result is a white line drawing on a black background. The glossy surface of scratchboard will also take pen lines.

SGRAFFITO—A technique used in ceramic decoration of greenware (unfired). It is done by cutting a design through a layer of paint or colored "slip," with a sgraffito tool, thus exposing the clay body underneath.

If you are doing a sgraffito decoration on a background consisting of several coats of paint, you may find the cutting a bit difficult. To solve this problem, dampen the background first (either by patting it with a damp sponge, or by covering the ceramic piece with a damp cloth for about fifteen minutes). Then go ahead with your sgraffito.

SPATTER—Spattering is an invaluable aid in decorating. Apply paint to a toothbrush and draw a comb through the bristles to make the spatters. Or if you don't mind getting paint on your fingers, do as I do, and draw your forefinger through the bristles. It is much easier to control the direction of the spatters this way. A spatter background will lend softness and depth to any design.

Enlarging a design by squares.

spattering a lamp shade

GLOSSARY
of Techniques

Spiral background of three colors on a ceramic plate. The design is then painted in two colors, plus black and sgraffito.

Sponging the edges of a ceramic cigarette box.

Example of even sponging.

SPRAY—A spray gun has always been the accepted way to spray paint, and for covering very large areas it is still the best. However, decorative spraying (around the edge or through the center) is much easier and less messy if you use the enamel spray cans now on the market. These come in all colors, including gold, and are a wonderful asset to decorating. Practice on newspaper first until you are familiar with this technique.

SPONGE—Sponging is most successful when used on ceramics. Apply paint to a fine textured sponge (available at your ceramic or art studio) and pat the sponge gently and evenly on the desired area. It is best to dilute the paint slightly before applying it to the sponge. This will help prevent your sponging from becoming too heavy or spotty. Practice on paper first until you are satisfied with your sponging technique.

SPIRAL—This ceramic technique is used as a background on circular or cylindrical objects.

Place the ceramic piece directly in the center of a decorating wheel or record player. If you are using a record player, stack enough old records on the player to provide an even base on which to place the plate or vase. To anchor your item securely, use wads of water-base clay.

Apply color to a fine-textured sponge. The "one stroke" paints are best for spiraling.

Start your wheel or player moving at a medium speed, place your sponge in the center (or top of upright items), and draw the sponge slowly toward you in a straight line. The sponge will leave spirals of color as it moves toward you. Use several colors for a more effective spiraling.

Because the greenware (unfired clay) absorbs the paint so quickly, you will probably have to repeat the process several times in order to get enough color in the spirals.

TRANSFER—Trace the design onto tracing paper. Place the tracing in the proper position, slip carbon paper or graphite paper underneath and transfer the design with a sharp pencil. If the background color is too dark to show carbon lines, use yellow or white carbon transfer paper (available at art stores).

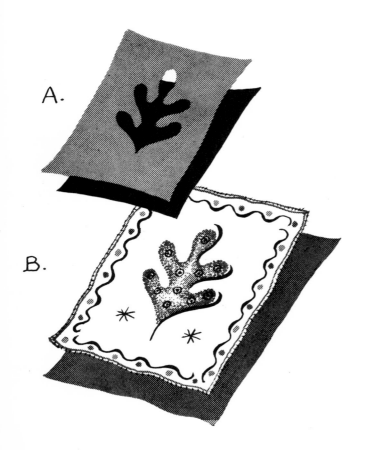

STENCIL—To make a stencil, use a piece of stencil paper large enough to allow at least 1″ around the outside of the design. Most stencil paper is transparent enough so that you can place it over the design and trace the main outlines with a sharp pencil. Or you can transfer the design with carbon paper. Cut out the traced outline with a stencil knife. The remaining part is your stencil.

SILK SCREEN PRINTING—This is a method of making color prints from a series of silk screen stencils. Each color of the design requires its own stencil and separate printing, so that when the process is completed you have a design with colors fitting together or overlapping neatly. All of the supplies for this process are obtainable at any art store.

There are various ways of preparing the stencils; one of the most popular is the tusche-and-glue method:

Paint the design for a color with tusche (a greasy black ink) directly on a piece of silk which has been especially woven for this purpose and tightly stretched on a wooden frame. Now, block out carefully with glue the areas not to be printed in that color. Remove the tusche with its own solvent—and you have one complete screen.

Prepare the screens for the other colors in the same manner. For printing, you will need what is called "silk screen process paint." The paint must be forced through the silk onto your paper, textile, wood, metal, glass, plastic or ceramic by means of a squeegee (a rubber blade encased in a wooden molding). After you put the paint inside your silk screen, make one stroke with the squeegee from end to end of the frame, applying as evenly as

(Top) Working stencil.

(Below) Finished stencil painting with hand touches added.

GLOSSARY
of Techniques

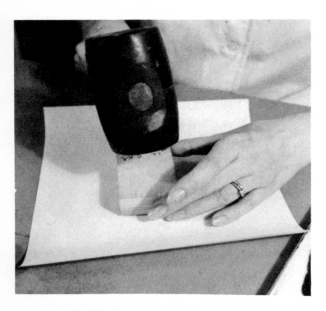

Tapping the back of the block with a wooden mallet to make a print.

possible. Lift the frame and the print has been made. Let the work dry and don't pile it up. After you have finished with a screen for the day you must clean it thoroughly.

Silk screen printing looks like block printing but will show the square lines of the silk weave if you look closely.

There are a number of books and booklets on the subject which go into greater detail than space allows here.

BLOCK PRINTING, always one of the most popular crafts, appeals to amateur and professional artists alike.

From a block print it is possible to produce book plates, greeting cards, wrapping paper, designed textiles, brochures, etc.

The mounted linoleum blocks painted white are best for all printing done on paper. They may be used on fabric too, although sheet linoleum is generally used for textile block printing, permitting the use of a larger design.

Paper for block printing should be absorbent. Rice paper is the best but you may use white or colored construction paper. (All block printing equipment is available at most art stores.)

You will need cutting tools, printing inks, rollers (preferably one for each separate color), and a sheet of glass for rolling out the ink.

Transfer the design to the linoleum block. Remember though, the design will be reversed when it is printed, so draw or trace the design on tracing paper, turn the paper over and use that side for transferring. After the design has been transferred to the block, ink in the design with India ink, especially if the design involves a lot of detail. Pencil lines may rub off or smudge.

Cut out all the areas you want left white. The uncut part will print the color. It is best to use a small "V" shaped tool to outline the design and a larger tool for the big areas.

After the block is cut, clean the surface with a stiff brush.

Spread a little printing ink on a glass sheet with a palette knife. (For fabrics add a few drops of textile medium to the ink.) Work the roller back and forth until the ink is smooth and thin on both the roller and glass, and then roll the color on the linoleum block. Place the inked block face down on your paper or fabric and press down by tapping the block with a wooden mallet or hammer. If you are blocking fabrics with sheet linoleum, stepping on the linoleum will make a good print.

For multi-color block prints, you must cut a separate block for each color.

Always place several layers of newspaper under the fabric or paper before you print.

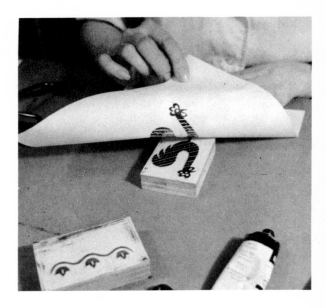

"Peeling" the print off the block.

PAPER AND GREETING CARDS

Receiving or sending a hand-made greeting card lends a wonderfully personal touch to any greeting. Also, applying designs to paper will give you good starting experience.

There are various ways to make your own cards, most of which are simple and effective.

The most popular method is the linoleum block print (see Pages 10 and 11). Since the block print combines semi-production with hand work, it is widely used by both amateurs and professionals. A few brush strokes of poster paint or glitter will add a great deal of interest to a print.

Or you can use **silk screen printing** if you intend to make a number of cards with the same design. Add personal touches later.

Another method of producing a large number of cards is by making a black-and-white line drawing and having it printed in quantities by a commercial printer. It is a fairly inexpensive process and one used by many professional artists. Consult your printer as to the best choice of paper for printing. Incorporate your own individual greeting in the original drawing.

A pen and india ink or **scratchboard** drawing will reproduce the most effectively. An unusual variation of a line drawing is **collage.** You can make very amusing family greeting cards using this method. Do not be afraid to experiment with fantastic ideas because the effectiveness of collage depends on originality.

You may prefer to concentrate on a smaller number of greeting cards to do entirely by hand.

A **spatter** technique used with a **newspaper mask** and a few brush strokes, is easy and the effect is striking for greeting cards, especially if you use silver or white for "snow."

Use poster paints and colored construction paper. Many different cards can be made from the same design by varying the spatter and background colors.

Children love to make this type of card and are invariably pleased with the professional result. It makes a good group project for schools, scouts, and clubs, of all sorts.

Add hand strokes, stars, and glitter. Glitter decorating is easy for children to manage. With the accompanying adhesive "pen" they are able to write their own greetings which would be difficult to do with paint.

Mount the hand-made part of your greeting cards on construction paper or tinted charcoal paper of a contrasting color.

Carl and Chris combine collage with a newspaper mask and a white spatter background for their greeting cards. They have added touches of glitter on the Christmas tree.

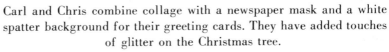

WOOD

The grain of the wood is used as a background for this cocktail tray.

Decorating on wood presents very few problems. You may choose any color for your background and any design, intricate or simple.

For a colored background, first apply two coats of fast-drying enamel (for a shiny finish) or flat wall paint (for a dull finish).

Whether you are using a painted background or just the raw wood, it is advisable (after applying any background **spatter** or **spray** work) to shellac the entire background before you transfer your design. Otherwise it is almost impossible to wipe off any mistakes, and in the case of a painted, spattered, or sprayed background, the background color may have a tendency to "bleed" through any paint applied over it. A coat of shellac will protect your background for further decorating.

After you have prepared the background, **transfer** your design and you are ready to paint.

For your paints, I suggest matt lacquers because they are easy to handle and dry almost immediately to a flat finish. These lacquers have a large range of colors, including gold.

You may also use enamels or tube oil paints, although they are not as easy to handle. If you use oil paints, add a fast-drying medium to speed up the process.

One of the most effective methods of decorating on wood is combining **newspaper masks** with a **spray** or **spatter** background. This method lends a very professional touch to any hand work. Use it often, you will find it very satisfactory. Give your finished ware a coat of glossy varnish or matt varnish (for a dull finish). A bar varnish is good for items that will receive a good deal of wear and tear (trays, salad bowls, table tops, etc.).

For an extra fine finish, hand rub with pumice powder.

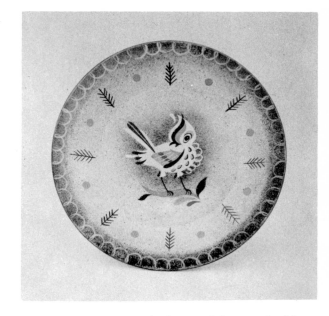

A wooden plate painted white and decorated with a newspaper mask and spatter. Hand strokes were added afterwards.

A wooden box painted black with a color spattered through the center to soften the simple design.

Burning a design on a suede jacket with an electric wood burning tool.

LEATHER

Painting on leather is one of the simplest forms of decorating. It requires only the leather itself as a basic background, and the consistency of leather is conducive to easy painting.

Leather book covers, belts, purses, wallets —all are wonderful items to decorate, especially for that "one of a kind" gift.

The simplest designs (particularly decorative initials) are best for leather decorating.

Since leather has a pleasing quality of its own, you will only want to embellish the leather and not overwhelm it with decoration. However, a very light **spatter** of color in the center of the leather item is often effective with an initial or a monogram.

Transfer your design directly to the leather (do any **spatter** work first though).

For your paints, new fast-drying matt lacquers are best. Although tube oil paints are not as easy to handle, they will work well on leather too. The oil paints are very good for items such as belts which bend a lot and may have a tendency to crack the paint after much wear. If you thin the oil paints with turpentine and use them almost as a wash you won't have cracking and peeling problems.

A very unique and interesting technique is burning a design in leather. Use a wood-burning tool, or electric "pen" such as is available in children's wood-burning kits. You will find this method particularly effective and easy to do on suede and other soft leather.

Practice first until you become familiar with the proper handling of the "pen" and keep your designs as simple as possible.

An Indian motif lends personality to a leather wallet.

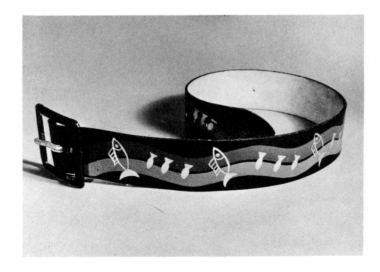

A stripe design used effectively on a leather belt.

GLASS

Painting on glass has become a very popular form of decorating. There is a large variety of glassware available, including ash trays, perfume bottles, hurricane lamps, drinking glasses, table tops, etc.

For purely decorative items, you can paint with enamels, tube oils, or lacquer. The glossy lacquers are particularly good for this type of decoration. They cover well and shine with the glass.

Using tube oil paints as a thin wash gives a transparent effect which is interesting on glass. This technique can also be applied to clear plastics.

For greater permanence on glass which will receive a good deal of wear and tear, paints that can be baked in a kitchen oven are available. (These paints are also suitable for glazed tiles and china. Ask your ceramic dealer about glass lustres and colors which require firing in a ceramic kiln.) This type of paint is completely permanent.

Choose simple designs for your glass decorating.

Transfer the design to the glass or simply fasten a tracing of the design to one side of the glass and then paint on the other side following the lines of the tracing.

Painting a design underneath the top of a glass table, tray, etc., or on the back of a glass cupboard door is a good idea for greater durability. But remember that your finished design will be reversed.

If a reverse decoration is not desirable, trace the design on tracing paper, turn the tracing over and pencil it again. Use this side, face down, for transferring. Then if you paint on the back of the glass the finished design will not be reversed when viewed from the front.

When painting on the back of glass begin your painting with the accents and any outlines or borders. Then paint the solid areas. If a background is desired, paint it last, going over the entire design. The reason for painting this way is that a color applied on top of another color will not show through from the other side.

The **spray** technique can be used as an accent for all glass painting, whether as a partial background or as an edging.

A decoration applied to the reverse side of the glass. An enamel spray can was used to spray the edges.

A simple design done with glossy lacquers over a light spatter background.

CERAMICS

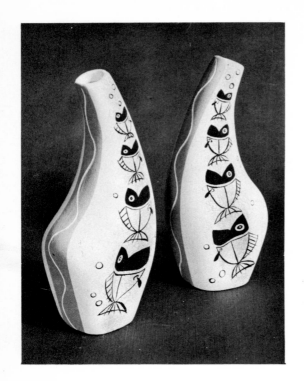

Sponging a color through the center of this cruet set lends depth to a simple line design.

Ceramic decoration involves painting on water-base clay which is then baked at a high temperature (of about 1850° F). After a glaze (a glass-like protective covering) is applied to the clay it is fired again. Because this must be done in a special ceramic oven (kiln) and requires colors (underglaze paints) prepared especially to withstand high heat, it would be wise to consult your ceramic studio for further information, if you are not familiar with ceramic procedures.

The designs in this book do not require any shading and will, therefore, adapt very nicely to underglaze painting.

When a decoration calls for a solid background, apply three coats of underglaze paint for good coverage. Dilute the first coat slightly and use the next two coats full strength. Always paint large areas with a large flat brush and alternate your strokes. That is, apply one coat of paint in one direction, the second in the opposite direction, etc.

There are a variety of decorating techniques available to the ceramist. Among the most effective and simple are **sponge, spatter,** and **spray.** They may be used for a decorative edging, or as a complete background for a simple design. Used as a background for **newspaper masks,** these three techniques are extremely interesting and almost infallible.

A **sgraffito** decoration is effective on a solid background. Choose a design consisting mainly of lines with perhaps one or two accents of color.

A **spiral** background is another technique often used in ceramics but is confined to circular or cylindrical objects. With this type of background use a fairly simple design with a few accents of **sgraffito.**

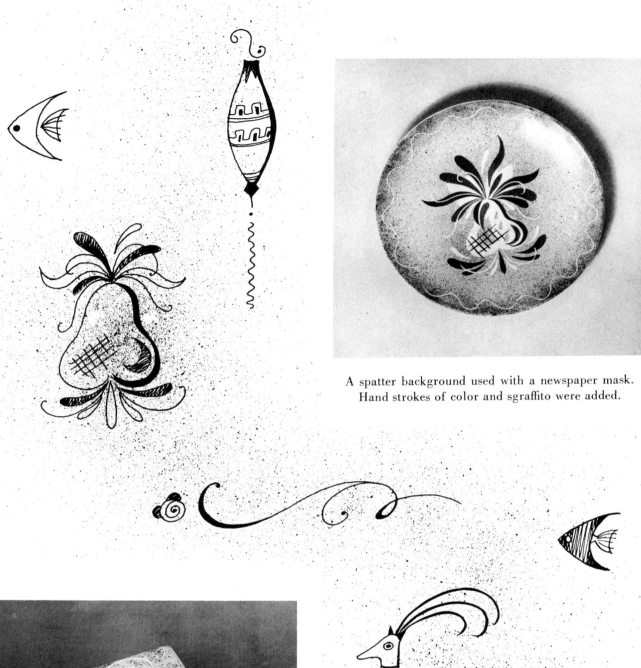

A spatter background used with a newspaper mask. Hand strokes of color and sgraffito were added.

Sgraffito design on a combination solid and sponged background.

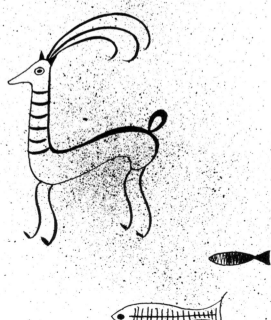

TEXTILES

A simple line design with a spatter background.

Hand strokes combined with a stencil painting.

When painting on textiles, limit yourself as much as possible to the light-colored fabrics. Dark colors will show through your paint, making the colors muddy. If you try to solve this problem by applying the colors more heavily a certain amount of stiffness will result.

Smooth textured fabrics, such as linen, cotton, nylon, silk, organdies, etc., will take color and detail much better than the rougher textured fabrics (wool or burlap).

Fasten your material to a flat board or table and put a piece of blotting paper under the fabric to soak up any excess paint. **Transfer** the design with a hard pencil but try not to get too heavy a line as it may show through the paint.

The paints prepared especially for textiles are the most satisfactory, although you may use the tube oil paints or some of the lacquers which will work on textiles. It would be a good idea to check with your art dealer as to the best paints available.

The lacquers are perfect for fiberglass or parchment lampshades and cloth-bound book covers. With them, you can use a **spatter** technique very effectively as a background for a simple line design. Spattering with the prepared textile paints is not as satisfactory because of the heavy consistency of the paint.

One of the best methods for decorating textiles is with a **stencil.** Because the stencil will determine the main part of your design, you need add only a few hand strokes for accent. A stencil painting without hand strokes is apt to appear mechanical and flat, so be sure to add hand touches.

When painting textiles with a stencil use a stiff stencil brush. Work with very little paint on your brush, scrubbing most of it off on paper before painting. Otherwise, your stenciling will be spotty and uneven.

Always paint in from the edge of the stencil working toward the center, and leaving a little space in the center of the design free of color. Work in a little shading of a darker color around the edge. This adds depth to a design.

Hand **blocking** and **silk-screening** (see Pages 9 to 11) are popular and effective methods of decorating textiles. They are particularly suitable for repeat designs, or where a quantity of one item is desired. With these methods, too, a few hand strokes will add great interest and color.

METAL

Painting on metal offers many possibilities for varied effects.

You may paint directly on copper or brass which will create a most unusual and unique type of decoration.

The black toleware available today in most art and hardware stores is perfect for any decoration that calls for a dark background.

Use enamels or flat wall paint for your colored backgrounds.

Use **spatter** and **spray** work freely on metal, either as a background for a simple design or as a decorative edging for a more intricate design. Before decorating on a painted background do all **spatter** or **spray** work first and then give the entire background a coat of shellac. This way any mistakes in decoration may be wiped off without destroying the background.

As soon as the background is ready for decorating, **transfer** the design. If you draw the design free-hand, a soft chalk is best on metal and will wipe off easily.

Your choice of paints is largely a matter of personal preference, as there are many paints suitable for designs on metal. The fast-drying lacquers are the easiest to handle. You may also use tube oil paints, but as the designs in this book do not require any shading, the lacquers are more satisfactory.

Combining a **spatter** background with **newspaper masks** is a most unusual and attractive method of decoration.

For a final finish on metalware, apply a coat of bar varnish. If you prefer a hand-rubbed finish, use **pumice powder.**

Black tole ware painted white with enamel and then spattered in two colors for a more interesting background.

White spatter and newspaper masks decorate a black tole tray.

Copper is used as the background for a Chinese design painted in flat lacquers.

PAINTED WALLS AND FURNITURE

Painting on walls and furniture offers a challenge to anyone interested in decorating.

The possibilities range from an ambitious mural to a small spot decoration on the back of a chair.

Beginners are often frightened when faced with a large expanse of wall to decorate. However, it is not necessary to cover a large surface completely with decoration. A small well-placed design, perhaps over a child's bed, or used as a repeat pattern to frame a door, is sometimes more effective.

After choosing a design, either **transfer** or draw it free-hand with a soft chalk on any smooth painted surface. Rather than try to transfer a design to a rough surface, such as a stucco wall, it is best to make a **stencil** and draw around it with chalk to get your guide lines for painting.

Use tube oil paints, enamels, or flat lacquers for your decorating. The lacquers are the easiest to handle and dry immediately to a flat finish (which is more attractive on walls and furniture than a glossy finish).

Children's rooms and furniture particularly appeal to all decorators. Here you can be as original and daring as you wish. Toy boxes, bureaus, walls, desks, and beds when decorated with Indian, Western, Circus, or Nursery designs will please any child. Apply a coat of varnish to your decorated furniture. For an extra fine finish hand rub it with pumice powder.

Window frames can be painted very effectively with a simple border.

Fruit, vegetables, and provincial motifs are appropriate for kitchen doors and cupboards.

Soften your decoration with **spatter** or **spray** backgrounds and edgings. **Spray** work is good for large areas which would take too long to **spatter.**

Don't forget exterior walls and doors. A handsomely decorated outside door lends individuality to any house. Garage doors and walls can also be very gay and decorative. Keep your designs large and simple. They are usually viewed at some distance and will not carry well if they are too small. You may want to **enlarge** your designs for this purpose. Use house trim paint for exterior surfaces.

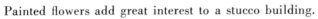

Painted flowers add great interest to a stucco building.

A simple border frames a window effectively.

HOW TO DEVELOP IDEAS FOR DESIGNS

SPRING

SUMMER

The planning of any creative project is extremely important and should be undertaken with great care. Although technical ability is important, of course, many wonderful techniques have been wasted on a poorly planned piece of work. Professional artists know from experience that time spent on careful planning is always time well spent.

Every project will require an individual treatment, depending on your object, the design motif, materials used, and the over-all approach to the work.

If you are not restricted to any particular theme, then you are free to choose whatever appeals to you personally and is appropriate for your purpose. Where the object to be decorated calls for a specific theme such as Christmas, Western, Music, etc., you have a limited choice of subject but you can choose a treatment.

Treatment is an important consideration. Undoubtedly "A rose is a rose is a rose," but a modern treatment of a subject will result in quite a different decoration than a traditional treatment of the same subject. Your approach can be modern, provincial, traditional, frivolous, or amusing—as you prefer.

Consider carefully the materials with which you will be working. If they involve techniques that are unfamiliar to you, don't handicap yourself with an intricate design. Keep your designing simple so that you are free to concentrate on technical problems.

A design that is suitable for one craft may have to be revised or simplified for another craft. Don't hesitate to revise a design to fit your particular purpose. This will lend individuality to any design. For example, you may have used a colorful spring landscape very successfully on a white background and obtained a gay, bright decoration. Try changing it to a snow scene on a subdued background for an entirely different effect. Remove the leaves on the trees, flowers, grass, and all other signs of spring. Then cover the ground, trees, and rooftops, with snow. Falling snow completes this scene and you have a brand new design.

Keep a file of your favorite designs and experiment with your own ideas of revision.

From one design it is possible to develop many variations resulting in an inexhaustible supply of designs.

It is a good idea to try out all designs and ideas with paper and pencil first.

Draw the shape of the object to be decorated (exact size if possible) on bristol board or drawing paper. I advise bristol board (available at art stores in student pads) because it is easier to handle for filing purposes

WINTER

AUTUMN

29

and a file of finished sketches is invaluable. Without such a reference, you might, over a period of time, forget a particularly good color scheme or a design you have successfully revised.

After the main shape has been drawn, place tracing paper over it and start experimenting with various designs, shifting them around until you find an arrangement that is pleasing. Take plenty of time (and tracing paper) with this because it is the most important step in decorating. Here you can bring in all your ingenuity and imagination. Don't try to force a design to fit when it obviously doesn't. If a design is too small for the area, try doubling it or using it as a series. This is usually very effective.

Apply the rules of addition and subtraction to your designing. Take something from one design and add it to another, make a border from a small part of a large design, or use a small design (stars, snowflakes, fish, etc.) in an all-over pattern. This is particularly effective on any odd-shaped object that is difficult to decorate. Use small fillers (wavy lines, stars, leaf sprays, etc.) freely where necessary. They do not have to mean anything in themselves as long as they add balance or interest to the over-all design.

When you have decided on the most satisfactory design possible, **transfer** it to the area you have drawn on the bristol board.

Now try out several color schemes (using layout or tracing paper) with water colors or poster paints. Choose the best one and apply it to the bristol board drawing. If you are going to use a **spatter** background now is the time to try it—or if you plan to use a **newspaper mask,** cut it out now (cut two at a time so you will have one for the final project) and use it on your drawing.

Wherever possible, apply to paper all the methods and colors you intend to use later. If you don't like the result, it is much easier and cheaper to throw away paper than a metal tray, ceramic vase, etc. On the other hand, if you do like the paper sketch, you will be able to loosen up and do a better job with the final decorating because you won't be plagued with doubts as to the success or failure of your work.

Experiment freely and often with ideas, designs, and techniques.

You may be disappointed at times, but trial and error will bring surprising rewards.

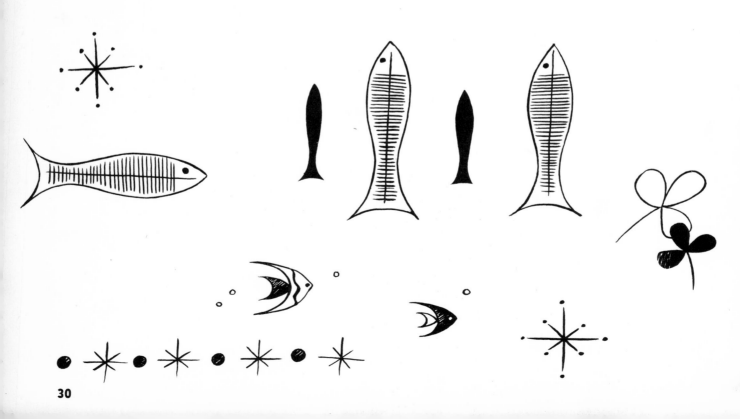

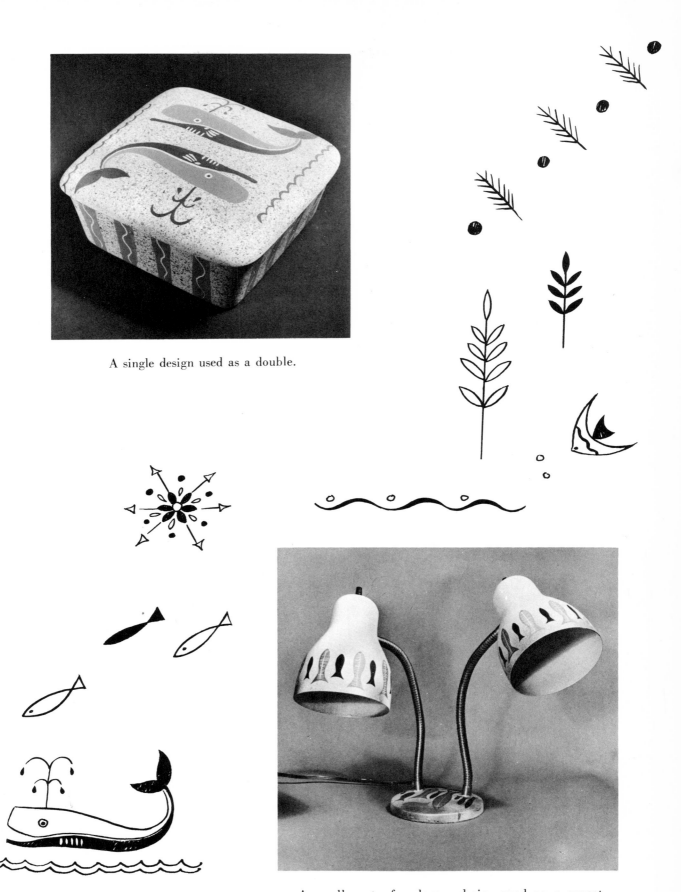

A single design used as a double.

A small part of a larger design used as a repeat border.

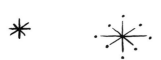

HOW TO START

After you have chosen the space to decorate and the design you want to put in that space, take a piece of tracing paper. Lay the tracing paper over the design and make a rough sketch of the design.

Let us suppose that you are using the design of the two chickens shown lower on this page. Trace the entire design and then take the tracing paper with the design on it and place it on your object. Center it in the space and see if it is the right size.

Scotch tape the tracing paper design onto your object in exactly the position you want, with carbon paper underneath it. Now go over the design with a pencil so that the carbon takes the impression onto the object. Remove the tracing paper and carbon when you are finished. You have now made a transfer.

Next step is to get your paints ready. Before you decide on your paints, you must look at the color guide which appears on the bottom of every double spread, and in this case, you can look at the color guide of the page below. You will note that one chicken is in gold and the other in black. The lighter cross-hatching indicates the gold and the darker color is the black. The white areas are indicated by the white square in the color guide. Of course the light areas will be added after you have your main colors down.

In the color guide you will find that the background is indicated in the color guide on the left. In one case your background may be white, and therefore what you leave unpainted will come through white unless you decide to add the white later. In another case you might find that the background is turquoise or you will have to paint the background first in turquoise. The colors that you are going to paint are determined more or less by the background color. The edges can be sprayed or spattered afterwards.

Following the same procedure, you can apply any design in this book using the color guide and sketches in the way outlined here.

COLOR GUIDE

color of object	gold	blue green	black	white
white	gold	blue	black	gold
spray or spatter edges black				
turquoise	white		black	

(Above) The author at work in her studio painting a fish design on a metal tray. (Right) Small ceramic mug decorated with Christmas design in three colors.

(Above) Small wooden plate, decorated in two colors of lacquers.

(Above) Painted wooden bread board using same motif.

(Right) The same African motif applied to a wooden box painted black and spattered with blue in the center. The design is painted over the spatter.

(Right) Large wooden platter painted first in red and white with enamels and then overpainted with the design.

(Below) Wooden cocktail tray first lacquered and then painted with the design. (Right) The wooden bread board for which newspaper mask and spatter background have been used. Details of the design have been added in flat lacquer afterwards.

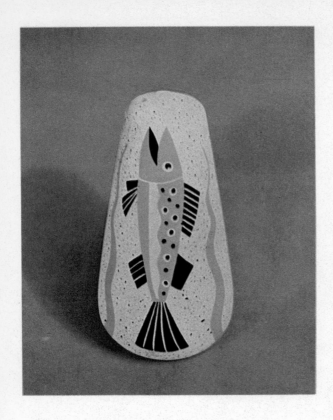

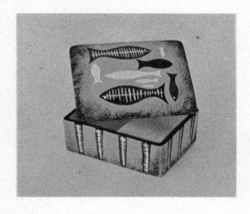

(Below) Ceramic cigarette box with background painted blue and then design painted in two colors in sgraffito.

(Above) Ceramic lamp base in bisque (unglazed) with spatter background and design painted in two colors in sgraffito. This should be glazed after the design, as should all ceramic objects.

(Right) Black tole tray with white spatter background and newspaper mask used for design.

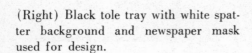

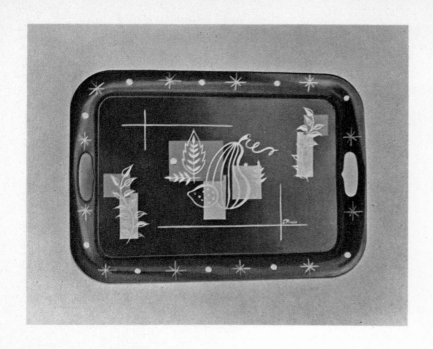

(Left) Black tole tray painted in three colors with flat lacquer. (Below) Small wooden plate painted white and newspaper mask used for design with spatter background.

(Below) Ceramic base with spiral background applied on potter's wheel or record player and design painted in two colors and gold.

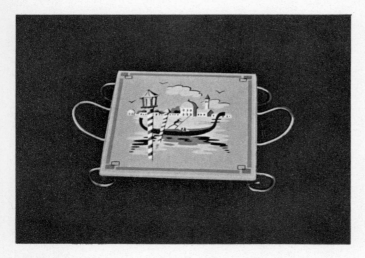

(Above) Ceramic tile in a brass trivet. The background was first painted and the design painted over it with underglazed paints.

(Below) Large metal tray of which the background was painted white first. Then the edges were sprayed black and the design painted in the center with a newspaper mask for the design and a spatter background.

(Below) Three copper canisters painted in two tones of blue and white in flat lacquers. A coating of shellac was put on afterwards.

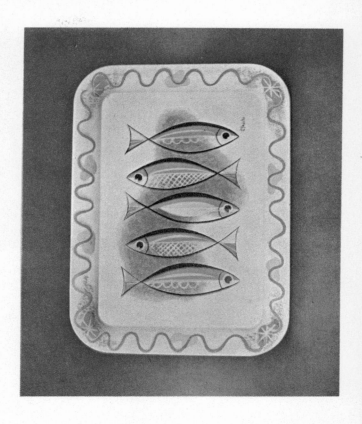

(Above) Metal tray, first painted white, sprayed with gold around the edges. Color was sponged through the center and design painted over. The border was painted last. (Right) This tray was painted in the same manner.

(Below) Black tole metal planter with dark red spattered through the center and design painted in gold, white and green.

(Below) Ceramic cigarette box with background spattered in rose and black. Then the design was painted in rose and black and sgraffito. A matte glaze was applied afterwards.

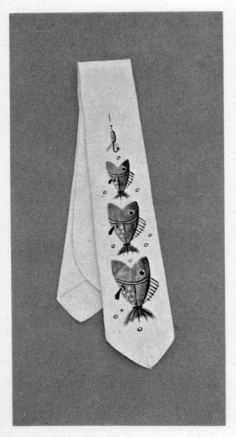

(Above) Linen luncheon napkins stencil-painted and hand touches added with textile paints.

(Above) Wool necktie stencil-painted with textile paints and hand touched.

(Below) White luncheon napkin with design painted in textile paints. Beneath is a small wooden plate with enamel background and the design painted in lacquers.

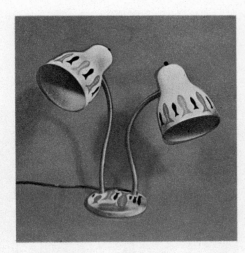

(Above) Metal desk lamp painted white with edges sprayed gold and design painted in three colors with flat lacquers.

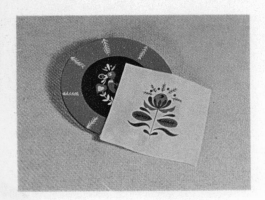

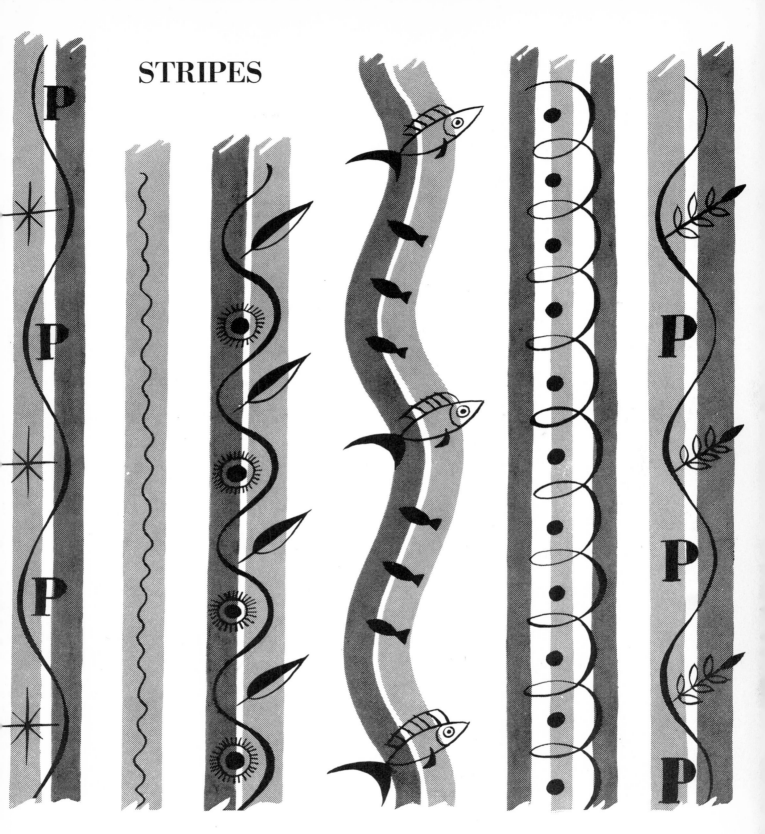

STRIPES

COLOR GUIDE

color of object			
white	rose	gray	black
blue green	brown	black	white

Metal tray.

DESIGNS
IN THE ROUND

Although this design involves six colors, the color areas are clearly defined and will not present any decorating problems.

COLOR GUIDE

color of object						
gray	pink	turquoise	dark red	dark green	black	white
y or spatter edges black						
black	yellow	gray	henna	blue green	gold	white

BORDERS

For a wavy line border on a square or rectangular object, break the line off at the corners.

An easy border for round objects—especially effective when applied on sprayed or spattered edges.

A simple wavy line can be varied in many ways.

FLOWERS

Ceramic ash tray.

COLOR GUIDE

color of object				
gray black	white white	turquoise gray	violet henna	black gold

Linen purse.

COLOR GUIDE

color of object					
yellow	white	turquoise	brown	black	gold
white	gray	turquoise	red	black	white

spray or spatter edges black

Fiberglass lamp shade.

PLANTS

COLOR GUIDE

color of object				
brown	gray	green	gold	white
white	turquoise	henna	black	gold
spatter henna through center				

Linen napkins.

FRUITS AND
VEGETABLES

COLOR GUIDE

FRUITS AND VEGETABLES

Wooden bread board.

COLOR GUIDE

color of object				
tan gray	white white	turquoise gold	brown red	black black

TREES

Leather photograph album.

COLOR GUIDE

color of object			
any color white *spatter brown through center*	white turquoise	gold brown	black black

Ceramic salt and pepper shakers.

INSECTS

COLOR GUIDE

color of object				
white	light blue	violet	black	white
spray or spatter gold through center				
black	pink	gray	white	gold

Ceramic salt and pepper shakers.

BIRDS

COLOR GUIDE

color of object	gray white *spray or spatter gold through center*	yellow turquoise	red brown	black black	white gold

Metal tray.

BIRDS

COLOR GUIDE

Ceramic cigarette box.

Ceramic cigarette box.

FISH

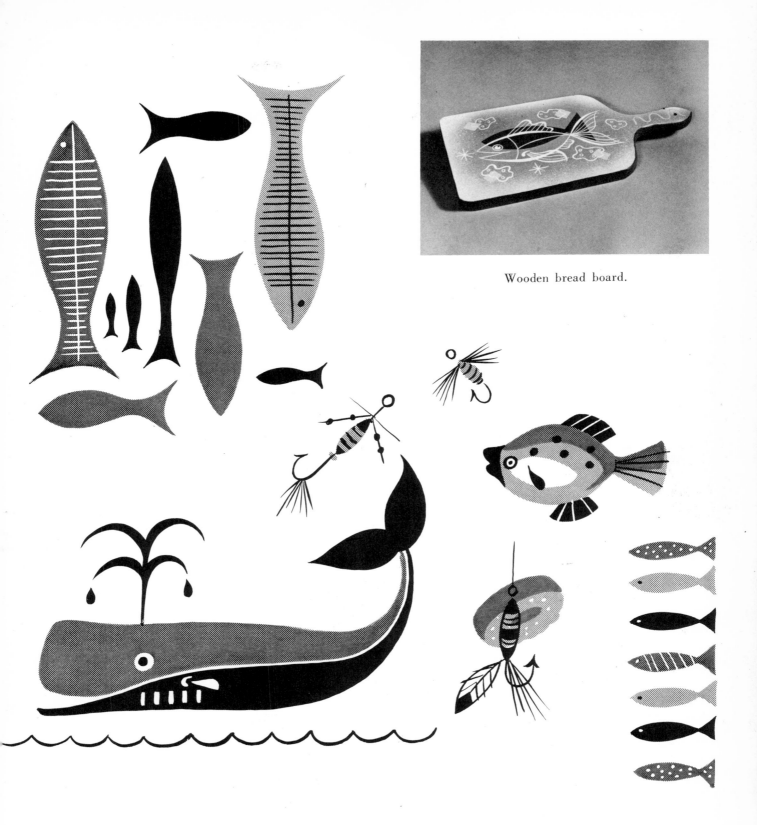

Wooden bread board.

COLOR GUIDE

color of object				
turquoise white *add red and black spatter*	henna gray	black red	white black	gold white

65

Ceramic lamp base.

FISH

COLOR GUIDE

color of object				
white	blue green	brown	black	white
add brown and black spatter				
black	turquoise	coral	white	gold

Leather purse.

ANIMALS

Would make an interesting repeat design.

COLOR GUIDE

color of object				
white	turquoise	brown	black	white
spray or spatter gold through center				
brown	white	gray	black	gold

A design easily adaptable to scratchboard.

COLOR GUIDE

color of object				
gray white	white gold	green red	black black	gold white

spray or spatter edges gold

Ceramic punch bowl.

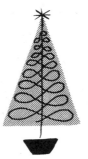

Could be an effective block print
with hand touches of gold.

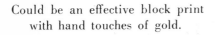

COLOR GUIDE

color of object				
white	gold	blue	black	white
spatter turquoise through center				
gray	black	red	white	gold

STILL LIFE

Black tole letter basket.

COLOR GUIDE

color of object				
black	yellow	turquoise	gold	white

spatter or spray henna through center

| white | gray | red | black | white |

SCENES

COLOR GUIDE

color of object					
white	light blue	gray	purple	black	white

spray or spatter edges blue green

| medium gray | light turquoise | yellow-brown | brown | black | white |

spray or spatter edges brown

SCENES

COLOR GUIDE

color of object					
white	turquoise	light brown	brown	black	white

spray or spatter edges brown

white	turquoise	gray	purple	black	white

spray or spatter edges black

Ceramic tile.

TRAVEL

CAFE

COLOR GUIDE

color of object	white gray	turquoise white	gray yellow	purple henna	black black	white gold

TRAVEL

Ceramic tile.

COLOR GUIDE

color of object	gray	yellow	brown	black	white
white					
spray or spatter edges brown					
black	turquoise	coral	purple	gold	white

AFRICAN

Small wooden plate.

color of object				
neutral or white	turquoise	henna	black	white
black	turquoise	gold	white	henna
spatter turquoise through center				

Ceramic tile.

CHINESE

Would make an interesting block print.

COLOR GUIDE

color of object					
white	gold	turquoise	blue green	black	white

spray or spatter edges black

| black | chartreuse | gray | henna | white | gold |

patter or spray gold through center

CHINESE

Black tole planter.

COLOR GUIDE

color of object	white	turquoise	blue	black
light brown	white	turquoise	blue	black
black	gold	green	henna	white

spray or spatter henna through center

Cotton polo shirt.

INDIAN

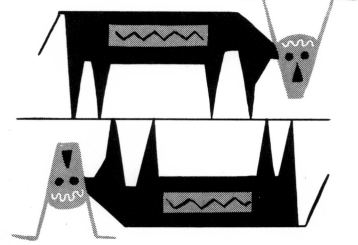

COLOR GUIDE

color of object				
brown white	turquoise yellow	coral blue	white black	gold white

WESTERN

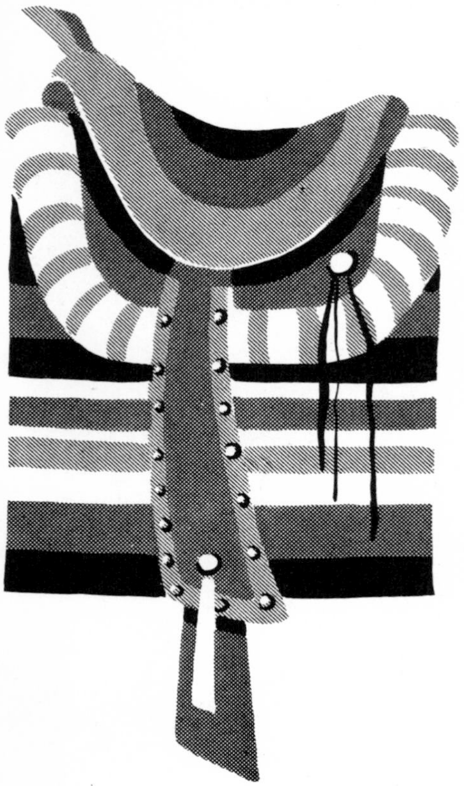

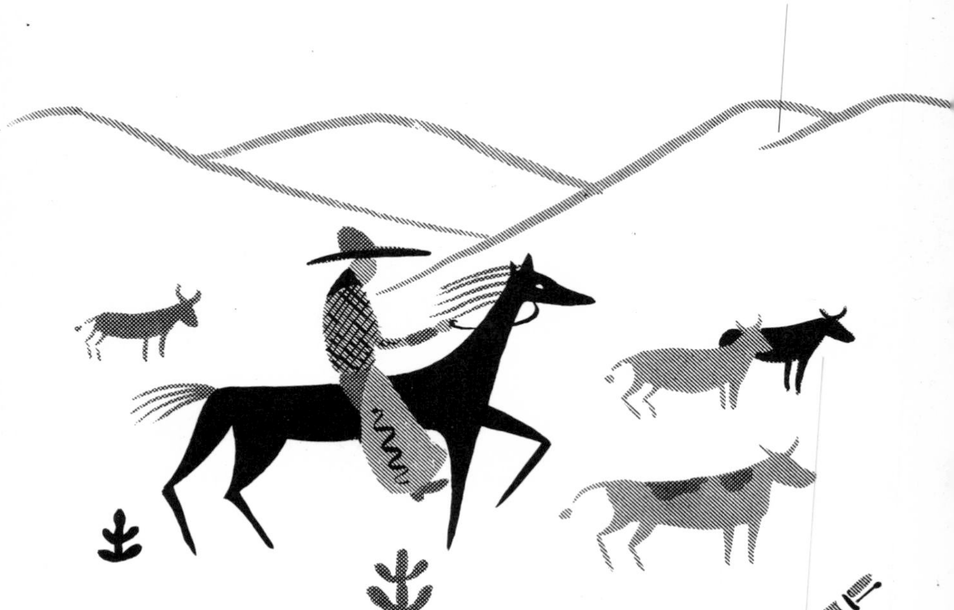

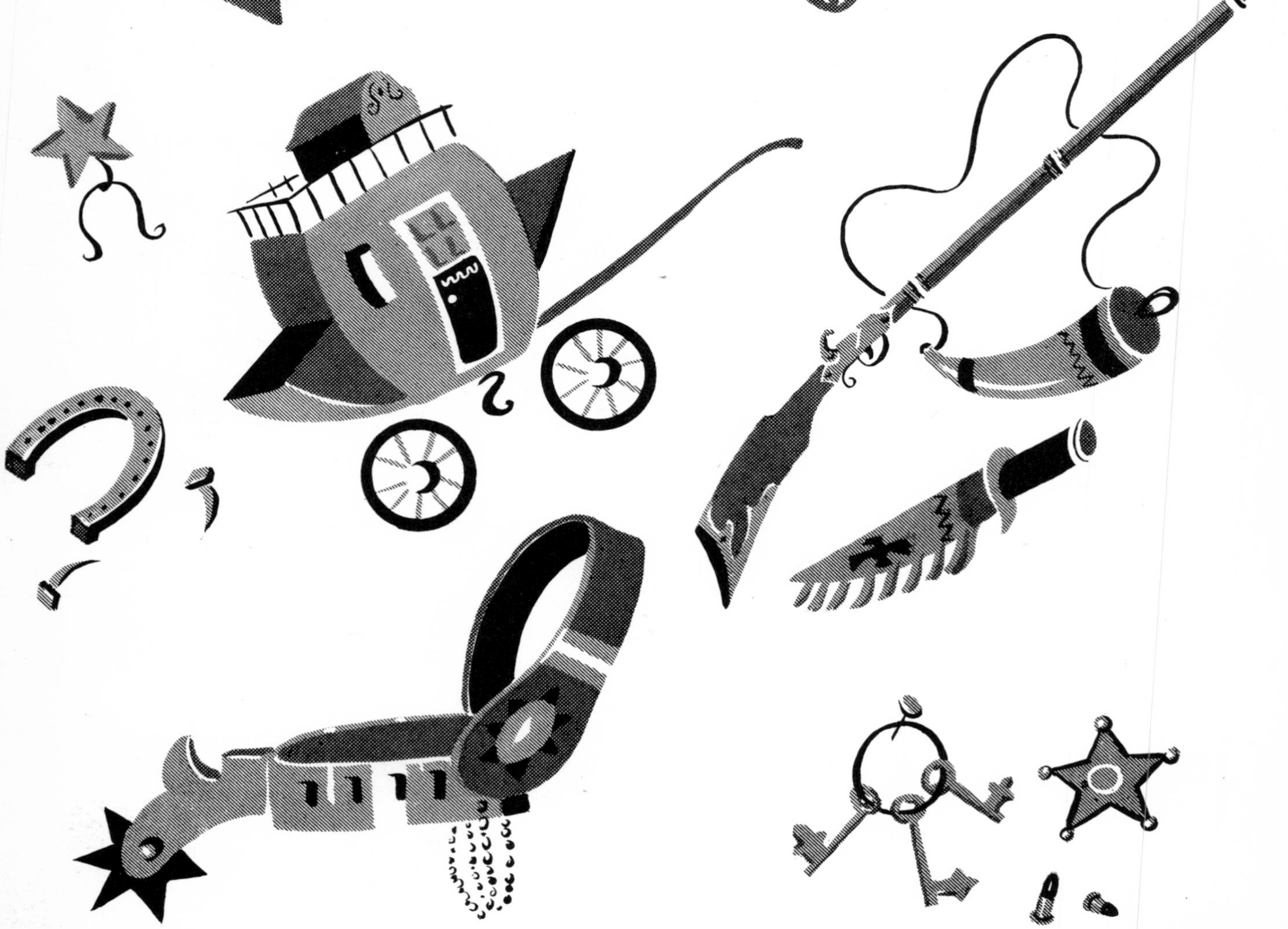

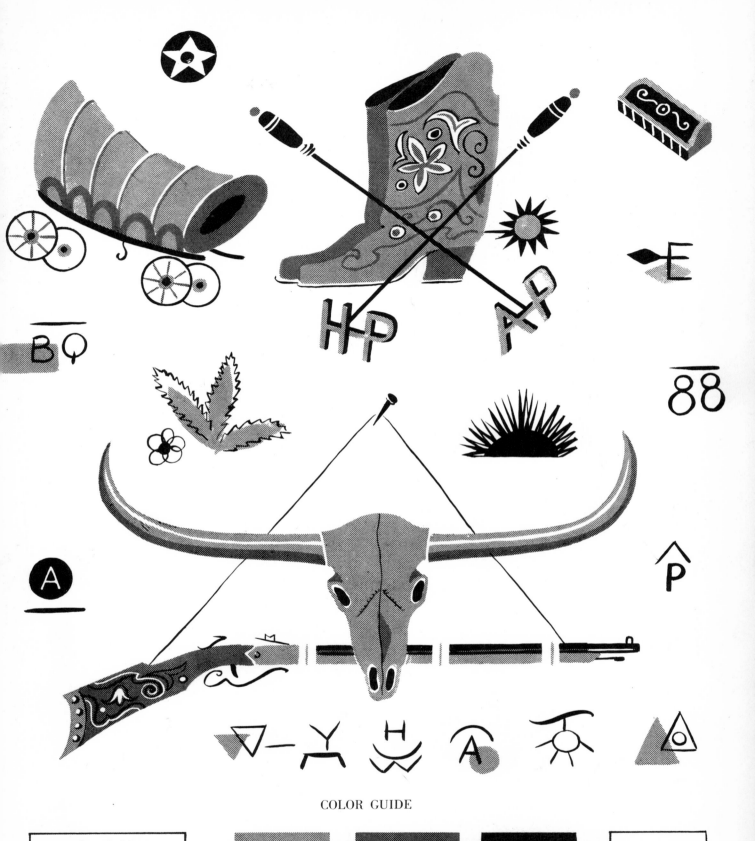

COLOR GUIDE

color of object				
yellow	white	turquoise	black	gold
white	gold	henna	black	white

Cotton napkins.

Ideal design for a stencil.

COLOR GUIDE

color of object				
white	gold	red	black	white
spatter black through center				
yellow	turquoise	brown	black	white

White luncheon napkin and small wooden plate

PROVINCIAL

COLOR GUIDE

color of object	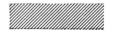			
	yellow	turquoise	brown	black	white
	black	red	gray	white	gold

Child's wooden stool.

COLOR GUIDE

color of object					
white	yellow	gray	brown	black	white
gray	white	turquoise	purple	black	gold

Small wooden plate.

COLOR GUIDE

color of object				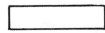
yellow	turquoise	brown	black	white
spray or spatter edges brown				
black	gray	red	white	gold

Large wooden platter.

PENNSYLVANIA DUTCH

Hex signs are effective on garage doors.

COLOR GUIDE

color of object			
white yellow	pink turquoise	gray brown	black black	white white

Leather record album.

MUSIC

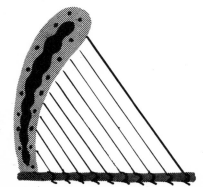

COLOR GUIDE

color of object				
white	gold	brown	black	white
red	white	gray	black	gold

ART

COLOR GUIDE

color of object					
white	gray	gold	purple	black	white
gray	white	turquoise	blue	black	gold

spray or spatter edges white

DRAMA AND DANCE

COLOR GUIDE

color of object					
white	gray	gold	red	black	white
gray	turquoise	white	purple	black	gold

HOBBIES

COLOR GUIDE

color of object				
white	gold	red	black	white
gray	pink	purple	black	white

COLOR GUIDE

color of object					
white	yellow	turquoise	brown	black	white
spray or spatter edges brown					
gray	turquoise	gold	red	black	white

KITCHEN

COLOR GUIDE

color of object					
white	gray	turquoise	purple	black	white
spray or spatter edges black					
turquoise	yellow	gold	brown	black	white

JUVENILE

Ceramic baby bowl.

Suitable design for a stencil or newspaper mask.

COLOR GUIDE

color of object				
white turquoise	pink gold	red henna	black black	white white

JUVENILE AND NURSERY

COLOR GUIDE

color of object					
white yellow	pink white	light blue turquoise	red brown	black black	white gold

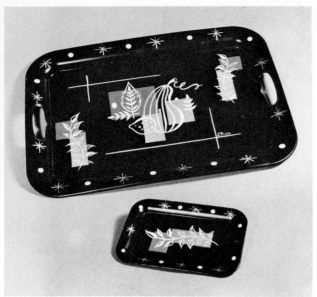

Black tole tray.

MODERN

COLOR GUIDE

color of object				
black gray	gold white	henna violet	green coral	white black

Glass top table.

MODERN

COLOR GUIDE

color of object				
white	gold	blue green	black	white
spray or spatter edges black				
turquoise	white	blue	black	gold

SPORTS

124

COLOR GUIDE

color of object				
gray white	white gold	turquoise henna	black black	gold white

SPORTS

COLOR GUIDE

color of object				

yellow white	gray gold	green brown	black black	white white

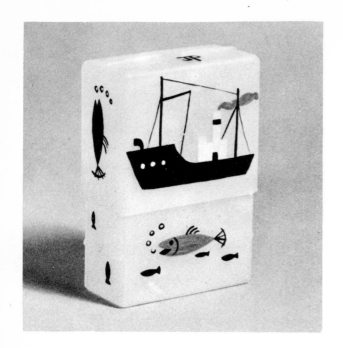

Plastic cigarette case.

NAUTICAL

COLOR GUIDE

color of object				
white	gold	blue	black	white
spray or spatter gold on edges				
turquoise	white	purple	black	gold

A B C D E F G
H I J K L M N
O P Q R S T U
V W X Y Z . ,

A B C D E F G
H I J K L M N
O P 2 R S T U
V W X Y 3 . .

Leather engagement book.

A small flower spray will soften any initial.

NOËL

POSTERS AND BROCHURES

ANTIQUES SHOW

T

FRANCE

World Air Lines

COMMUNITY PLAYERS

B e

A

B

COLOR GUIDE

color of object				
white	red	gold	black	white
yellow	turquoise	brown	black	white

All the materials mentioned in this book are available at art supply, ceramic supply, or hardware stores. However, if you have difficulty in obtaining the materials you may write to the manufacturer whose name is listed below and he can supply you, either with the product or with the name of your nearest dealer:

Block printing ink

Prang Printing Inks—The American Crayon Company of Sandusky, Ohio and New York City

Flat lacquers

Flo-Paque Paints—Floquil Products, Inc., New York 23, N. Y.

Glossy lacquers

Prang Dek-All Paints — The American Crayon Company of Sandusky, Ohio and New York City

Spray cans

Krylon Spray—Krylon, Inc., Philadelphia 46, Pa.

Poster paints

Rich Art Poster Paints—Rich Art Color Co., Inc., New York City

Textile paints

Prang Textile Colors—The American Crayon Co. of Sandusky, Ohio, and New York City

Silk screen supplies

Arthur Brown & Bro., 2 West 46th St., New York City, or,

Screen Process Supplies Mfg. Co., 508 W. MacArthur Blvd., Oakland, Calif.

Ceramic underglaze paints

Ceramichrome Ceramic colors and glazes —Ceramichrome Laboratories, Los Angeles 47, Calif.

Tru-Tone colors — Re-Ward Laboratories, 1985 Firestone Blvd., Los Angeles 1, Calif.

Ceramic tiles

Wheeling Tile Co., Wheeling, W. Va.

Ceramic tiles, trivets, frames

Soriano Ceramics Inc., Long Island City 5, N. Y.

General ceramic supplies

B. F. Drakenfeld & Co., 45 Park Place, New York City, or,

S. Paul Ward, Inc., 601 Mission St., South Pasadena, Calif., or,

Specialized Ceramics Corp., 200 W. Third St., Plainfield, N. J.

Recommended books

Artists' Manual for Silk Screen Print Making by Harry Shokler, Tudor Publishing Co., 221 Fourth Ave., New York City

The Complete Book of Pottery Making by John B. Kenny, Greenberg: Publisher, New York 22, N. Y.

INDEX

INDEX (Continued)